THE SCOTTISH HIGHLANDS

by Elisabeth Fraser

My heart's in the Highlands, my heart is not here;
My heart's in the Highlands, a-chasing the deer;
A-chasing the wild deer, and following the roe –
My heart's in the Highlands wherever I go.

Robert Burns

Contents

JARROLD

Introduction

The Scottish Highlands contain some of the finest scenery in Europe, yet this vast region, which covers almost two-fifths of Scotland, is for the most part sparsely populated. Geographically the Highlands Boundary fault line, which was formed 400 million years ago by the action of the earth's crust splitting and folding, left a distinct division between the Highlands and Lowlands of Scotland; in the Highlands, erosion of the ancient rocks by rivers and glaciers helped to create the region's wild appearance and character. This division, by the nature of its terrain, eventually produced a widely different way of life for the Highlander and the Lowlander. This Highland Boundary fault line lies diagonally across Scotland: commencing north of the Isle of Arran, then crossing the sea to Helensburgh and on through Aberfoyle to Comrie, Blairgowrie and Edzell, ending at Stonehaven. Everything north of this fault line is generally accepted as the Scottish Highlands, although some part of the eastern Highlands are quite flat.

Some of the greatest mountain masses in Great Britain are situated in the Scottish Highlands, and over 500 of the summits are at least 3,000 feet (900 m) high. Ben Nevis, in the Lochaber region, is the highest peak and rises to 4,406 feet (1,343 m). Most of the mountainous areas are to the west of the Highlands, although the largest concentrated ranges, the Grampian and Cairngorm mountains, are situated in a more central and eastern belt. In the winter, many of the higher mountains are covered in snow, which melts in spring, rushing and foaming down over waterfalls, crevices and gullies into rivers and lochs. It is this combination of lochs and mountains that gives such grandeur to the Scottish Highlands, providing a magnificent background for the many striking sunsets which dominate the sky with their deep oranges and reds, the remote snow-capped mountain peaks reflecting exquisite pinkish hues.

The Highlands are famous for their lochs, and it is possible to drive around many of the longer ones. There is a 77-mile (123 km) trip round Loch Awe, for example, starting and finishing at Taynuilt, near Oban, which uses several lesser-known roads and passes through some of Argyll's finest scenery. Loch Lomond has the largest surface area of the Scottish lochs, being 23 miles (37 km) long and 5 miles (8 km) at its widest. Along its banks are many wooded areas and thirty-three small isles, with mountains on both sides. Sometimes, the reflection of the mountains in the still waters of the loch is so sharp and clear that it is difficult to tell which is the real thing! The deepest loch is Loch Morar (1,017 feet/305 m), and its famous white sands can be seen on the way to Mallaig. Loch Ness has a recorded depth of 700 feet (210 m), although it is believed to be much deeper. It is approximately 24 miles (38 km) long, with an average width of 1 mile (1.6 km) and a volume of 265,000 cubic feet (7,504 cu m). Loch Ness is indeed formidable, it is in its murky depths that the Loch Ness Monster is supposed to hide. As well as the inland lochs there are many sea lochs; Loch Linnhe, on the Great Glen fault line (formed at the same time as the Highlands Boundary fault line), penetrates further inland than most other sea lochs.

Adding to the splendour of the Highland scenery is the wildlife. Red deer, wild goats and wildcats, otters, badgers, pine martens, dolphins and seals can still be found in the wild. In the remoter mountainous regions there are golden eagles,

buzzards and ospreys, and recently the fish eagle has begun to nest again. For thousands of years following the Ice Age, much of the Highlands was covered in forests of native broadleaf trees and Scots pine, and lynx, wild pigs, moose, reindeer, bears and wolves were typical of the wildlife. They disappeared as the forests were progressively cleared over the centuries by man, grazing animals and fire. The Forestry Commission was set up in 1919 to reverse the clearance procedure and ensure that large parts of the Highlands were forested for future generations. Recently, reindeer were reintroduced into the Cairngorm Mountains and are thriving; some are almost pure white. Special guided tours are available.

The coastline of the Scottish Highlands varies considerably. For example, in the Western Isles the golden sandy beaches are a sheer joy to experience, with interesting walks along remote shores, where grey seals dive and tumble in the deep waters. They pop their heads out of the sea and bark at one another, or wobble onto the rocks that jut out of the sea,

their skins gleaming in the sun, blending so well with the rocks that it is hard to see them. On the mainland, the western coast is punctuated by numerous sea lochs, and at times sheer drops to the sea below are visible. The road may perch on the top of the cliffs, then descend dramatically to sea level, or it may run inland for several miles before suddenly turning towards the sea again, to reveal a delightful sandy bay far below an immense rocky verge. There are tremendous rocky coastlines too, such as at Duncansby Head near John o' Groats in Caithness, in the extreme north-east of the Highlands. Here, one can walk by the cliffs and see the jagged sides of the deep gullies, with their hidden caves, and the huge protruding pinnacles that rise sharply out of the sea, called the Stacks. The rock ledges are full of screaming sea birds fighting for a place on which to perch.

Fort William and Ben Nevis from Loch Linnhe

The Highlanders, whose native tongue is Gaelic, were at one time under clan domination; each clan had its own chief and territory. Over the years, much of this has changed, but not the pride of belonging to a clan and retaining its name. Descendants of Scots come from all over the world to seek their ancestry, visit their clan territory and discover their 'homeland', as they still call it, even though generations have elapsed. One of the great events for Highlanders is the Gaelic festival known as The Mod, which is held in a different part of Scotland each year, organised by An Comunn Gaidhealach. Many of the old songs have a striking appeal, particularly when sung by Gaelic singers, who have a depth and clarity of singular beauty in the lilt of their voices.

Before the Jacobite Rebellion of 1745, the Highlanders' lifestyle was very different. There was a much larger population, and for the most part people lived in self-supporting crofting communities. The crofters were tenants of the clan chiefs, who owned the land, and they lived in cottages known as Black Houses, because of the central peat fire that blackened the insides. These were single-storey thatched cottages built of stone, containing quarters for animals too. The crofters reared cattle and sheep on the mountains and moors and cultivated oats and other crops on the lower slopes by means of 'lazy beds', a form of terracing – evidence of these bygone days can still be seen in the Highlands today.

Over the years, changes took place in land ownership and estate management. In the early nineteenth century, for example, there was an increase in the demand from England for wool. The clan chiefs, not wanting to miss out on the remunerative possibilities, sought ways to increase their sheep-rearing. Unfortunately, much of their land was divided among crofting communities, but unscrupulous landowners, seeking to become rich, totally disregarded the crofters' tenancy rights and drove them off the land into exile. This cruel period in Highland history is known as The Clearances.

However, today there are still crofters in the remoter parts of the Highlands, particularly in the islands, who continue to spin and weave and croft their lands – their crofting rights now protected by law. Crofters have also retained the right to cut peat to heat their homes, and often heaps of it can be

Striking sunset over Iona

seen drying by the roadside. To smell burning peat in the air is a unique aspect of the Highlands.

The construction of several major road bridges (the Forth, Tay and Friarton bridges) in the 1960s enormously improved the eastern approaches to the Highlands. The Ballachulish, Kessock, Kylesku and Dornoch bridges, along with numerous causeways, have further transformed communications to all areas. Yet another bridge is planned to cross the sea loch, Loch Alsh, joining the Isle of Skye to the mainland.

This is a far cry from 1724, when General Wade was sent up from London to develop better communications in the Highlands, and to help prevent further uprisings against the Hanoverian monarchy. At this time only trails and drove roads existed in the Highlands; drove roads were used to drive cattle and sheep to market. General Wade had a formidable task before him. He began in 1724 by rebuilding Fort William, then built Fort Augustus and Fort George; the latter is the only one left today, and it is truly magnificent. Linking roads were constructed, followed by more roads and bridges. After General Wade left Scotland, Thomas Telford added many more roads in the early nineteenth century. However, his chief engineering feat was the Caledonian Canal, which follows the length of the Great Glen fault line, extending from Inverness in the north-east to Loch Eil near Fort William in the south-west. The total length of the canal is more than 60 miles (96 km). Lochs Lochy, Oich and Ness are linked together by 21 miles (33 km) of artificial waterways with twenty-nine locks. One series of eight locks, lying between Corpach and Banavie, is called Neptune's Staircase. During the early part of the canal's history, provision was made for ships from the Atlantic to take a shortcut through to the North Sea; fishing fleets still do this today. It is also a challenge to yachtsmen, who are able to enter the canal from Loch Linnhe and sail along this unique waterway, enveloped in serenity and unforgettable beauty.

The very name Scottish Highlands may evoke romantic images of snow-capped mountains, kilted lairds, baronial castles, shaggy Highland cattle or wild moorlands covered in heather, yet it is impossible to find the total of its many aspects in one area. This small book, however, gives a taste of what there is to discover.

Reflections in Loch Lomond

Loch Lomond at Balmaha

Morning at Urquhart Bay, Loch Ness

A buzzard perches on a Highland hilltop

'White' reindeer in the Cairngorm Mountains

A remote, sandy beach on South Harris

The dramatic Highland coastline at Duncansby Head, near John o' Groats

The 'black house' at Arnol, Lewis

Crofters marking sheep on South Uist

The oldest croft house on South Uist, with Lochboisdale beyond

The Forth Rail Bridge made the Highlands more accessible in the nineteenth century

Kessock Bridge, linking Inverness to the Black Isle

The simple design of Kylesku Bridge, near Kylestrome, complements the surrounding unspoilt landscape

Tay Bridge at Dundee, a gateway to the Highlands

An aerial view of Fort George, near Nairn

Piper at Blair Castle, Blair Atholl

The Grampian and Cairngorm Mountains

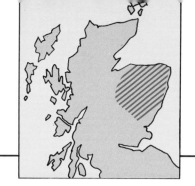

The Grampian mountain range meets the Cairngorms near Aviemore. This is a vast mountainous area, often wild and desolate-looking, but in fact teeming with life. It is one of the few remaining unspoilt parts of Scotland where the majestic Caledonian pine forest survives. In 1954 nearly 100 square miles (250 sq km) of the higher Cairngorms passed from the Rothiemurchus Estate, owned by Grant family, into the care of the National Nature Reserve.

There are several ski slopes in the region, which attract great crowds especially when weather conditions are good. The largest ski area is near Aviemore on the edge of the northern Cairngorm Mountains. The ski season lasts from December to May, but the Second Stage Cairngorm Chair Lift, rising 3,600 ft (1,100 m) above sea level, is open all year round. The Lecht Ski Centre is on the road to Tomintoul from Braemar, and the Glenshee Ski Centre is situated at the summit of Cairnwell Pass in the Grampian Mountains. Previously, the road from Blairgowrie through to the Grampians was very dangerous, especially at the Devil's Elbow, so-called because of a sharp bend that was hair-raisingly steep and treacherous, but in recent years the 'elbow' has been cut off to make a much safer ascent to the Cairnwell summit. From the summit the road continues to Braemar, famous for the Royal Highland Games held there every year which are attended by the Royal Family.

Balmoral Castle at Crathie is the Highland home of the Royal Family. It was purchased in 1852 by the Prince Consort for Queen Victoria, who fell in love with the beauty and grandeur of the countryside during one of her visits to Scotland. The route from Braemar to Aberdeen thereafter became known as 'Royal Deeside'. Balmoral Castle is open to the public at certain times of the year, when the Royal Family is not in residence.

There are several other interesting castles open to the public in this area, and the National Trust for Scotland has taken many into its care, such as Craigievar Castle, 26 miles (41 km) west of Aberdeen, Crathes Castle and Drum Castle near Banchory. Braemar Castle, once the home of the Earls of Mar and later a government barracks, is now owned by the Farquharsons of Invercauld and is well worth visiting. The picturesque parish church at Crathie, where the Royal Family worship when they are in residence at Balmoral Castle, is also open to the public.

The road to Tomintoul, which is the region's highest village, is one of the wildest and most mountainous in the Scottish Highlands. In the winter months the road is frequently closed because of heavy snow, but it is soon opened again to accommodate the ski parties that flock to the Lecht Ski Centre. During August, when the heather is blooming, nothing touches the heart more deeply than this purple hue stretching for mile after mile over the mountains, its richness dominating the landscape, the colour harmonising so perfectly with the grey of the rocks.

Tomintoul is part of the Whisky Trail, a major tourist attraction of recent years which covers a wide area of Speyside. Many distilleries are open to the public, and nearly all of them offer a 'wee dram' to visitors once they have been shown round and seen how whisky is produced. Grantown-on-Spey, near Tomintoul, is a favourite place to stay for those who love fishing and mountain climbing.

East of the Grampians is Aberdeen, the 'granite city' of the north, which has by far the most interesting architecture in the Scottish Highlands, and many very old buildings. Since the oil boom Aberdeen has developed considerably, although fishing has always been a major industry. Tourism, too, has increased over the years. Besides being a direct link by P&O shipping line to the Shetland Isles and Fair Isle, Aberdeen commands a central position for Royal Deeside, the Whisky Trail and the Castle Trail. (There are more castles in the area surrounding Aberdeen than anywhere else in the Highlands, and many are open to the public.)

South-west of Aberdeen, at Banchory, the B974 takes you across wild mountains and moors, which are carpeted in purple heather in late August. The road leads past Fettercairn to Edzell, where there is a byroad on to Kirriemuir, the birthplace of James Barrie, author of *Peter Pan*. Only a few miles to the south is Glamis Castle (open to the public), where the Queen Mother spent much of her childhood.

The Devil's Elbow, on the road through Glen Shee to Braemar, as it was before it was straightened out

Skiers in the Cairngorms
The salmon-rich River Dee, near Balmoral Castle

Craigievar Castle, near Alford, is crowned by fairytale turrets

An autumnal view of Balmoral Castle, the Highland home of the Royal Family

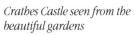

Crathes Castle seen from the beautiful gardens

The parish church at Crathie, attended by the Royal Family when they are in residence at Balmoral Castle

The dignified façade of Braemar Castle

Typical Cairngorms scenery in August – miles of purple heather overlooked by misty mountains

Dallas Dhu Distillery, near Forres, is a preserved time capsule of the Scotch whisky distiller's craft and is open to the public

Union Street, Aberdeen, preserves much of the city's original character

The ruins of Edzell Castle have ancient monument status
The Queen Mother spent much of her childhood at Glamis Castle, seen here

Loch Lomond and the Trossachs

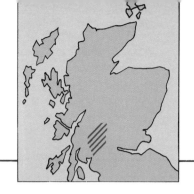

Sir Walter Scott's *Lady of the Lake* (published in 1810) and *Rob Roy* (1818) were undoubtedly responsible for making the Trossachs so popular, and the area has remained so ever since. But land ownership has changed considerably since Sir Walter Scott penned those famous novels. Today the Forestry Commission is by far the largest landowner in the Trossachs; the whole area comes under the umbrella of the Queen Elizabeth Forest Park, stretching as far as Rowardennan on the east side of Loch Lomond, including the whole of Loch Ard, Loch Achray and Strathyre west of Loch Lubnaig. Recently the Commission has added more land to the park.

Over the years the Forestry Commission has developed two major plans: a conservation plan, to protect, monitor and provide information on all wildlife in the area so that it is affected as little as possible; and a recreation plan, to develop and encourage care of the Commission's waymarked walks, camping sites and picnic areas. The Commission's greatest concerns are fire and erosion of the waymarked paths. The plans are constantly being updated to ensure maximum conservation and to give greater enjoyment to the ever-increasing number of visitors who seek the solace of these beautiful forests and hills. For more active walkers there are four waymarked Bens to explore: Ben Venue, Ben Ledi, Ben An and Ben Lomond - all a joy to climb with superb views from the summits. Allow an early start for such a venture, particularly the arduous climb of Ben Lomond. For those who prefer gentler walks, the forests are a sheer delight, with wild flowers, a great variety of birds, and occasionally a timid deer appearing from its mountainous retreat.

The Queen Elizabeth Forest Park Centre is near Aberfoyle, and is reached by a winding road from Callander over the Duke's Pass. In 1960 the Forestry Commission was given the purpose-built visitors' centre by the Carnegie Trust, for public enjoyment. At that time it was called the David Marshall Lodge, after the president of the Trust. Andrew Carnegie was born in Dunfermline, emigrated to America and made his fortune as a steel magnate, but he never forgot his homeland, setting up the Carnegie Trust for benevolent purposes.

The Strathclyde Regional Council Water Department owns 27,000 acres (11,000 ha) of land in the Trossachs, including Loch Arklet, near Stronachlachar, and Loch Katrine, where there is a visitors' centre and tearoom. It is at this end of the loch that the Water Department runs its 'screw steamer', the *Sir Walter Scott*, for cruises down to Stronachlachar. The *Sir Walter Scott* is a steam vessel maintained to a very high standard. It runs on smokeless fuel and is environmentally friendly in that it is non-polluting and has no detrimental effect on the water in Loch Katrine. In 1855 an Act of Parliament decreed that Loch Katrine should be retained as a catchment area for the city of Glasgow's drinking water. A dam was built to raise the level of the water, which was later raised twice more by a 1919 Act of Parliament. It is interesting to note that the water runs solely by gravity through pipes to Milngavie near Glasgow.

In the late 1940s the City of Glasgow purchased from the Earl of Ancaster the estate surrounding Loch Katrine, consisting of Brenachoile Lodge, several farms and numerous cottages. This beautiful estate is carefully maintained by the Water Department of Strathclyde Regional Council, which is now one of the largest sheep farmers in Scotland. No cars are allowed except for access; no pleasure boats are permitted on the loch;

Loch Ard, with snow-covered Ben Lomond beyond

there is no forestry in the area (although there are native trees), because large numbers of trees would be a drain upon the water; and fishing is limited and strictly by permission. Walkers are welcome to enjoy the exquisite beauty of the estate, for the lovely Loch Katrine is unsurpassed. It may not be as long as Loch Lomond nor as deep as Loch Ness, but it has a quality that expresses to those who come to share its peace and beauty the need to respect what it has to offer.

Loch Lomond's main A82 road runs from Glasgow all the way up the west side of the loch to Ardlui, and on to Crianlarich and Tyndrum. However, there is a lesser-frequented road on the east side running from Drymen as far as Rowardennan. At this point the West Highland Way walk continues to the end of the loch, where the Falls of Falloch are to be found, and on to Crianlarich, Tyndrum and Fort William, where it finishes.

Another scenic byroad runs from Aberfoyle to Stronachlachar, then continues by an unmarked wooded road to Inversnaid Hotel on Loch Lomond, where the views are magnificent. Between Inversnaid and Rowardennan towers the mighty Ben Lomond, overshadowing the whole area. There are many boat trips from Balloch that give panoramic views of Loch Lomond.

Callander is a thriving historic town close to the Trossachs and the nearby Falls of Leny. A Rob Roy and Trossachs visitors' centre has been opened here, run by the Loch Lomond, Stirling & Trossachs Tourist Board. Here the visitor can learn all about Rob Roy MacGregor, whose birthplace lies at the head of Loch Katrine at Glengyle, and decide whether this great Scottish character was a villain or a hero. From Callander the A84 leads to Lochearnhead, a favourite centre for water sports, and it is here that the road meets the A85 coming from Crieff, a delightful rural town where there is much to see, including a glass factory and the original Portobello Pottery Company; there is also a fine whisky distillery near Crieff worth visiting.

The A85 continues through Glen Ogle to Killin, where the famous Dochart Falls are to be found, tumbling over boulders and huge rocks. After heavy rain it is an unforgettable sight, especially if there is snow lying on the top of Ben Lawers, when the whole scene is quite magical. It is easy to lose all sense of time whilst standing on the ancient bridge over the falls, listening to the relentless, thundering noise of the water.

Beyond Killin there are two scenic byroads. The first leads to Glen Lochay, and the second goes over the mountains to Glen Lyon, near the National Trust for Scotland's Ben Lawers Centre. Glen Lyon is a most attractive unspoilt area where great herds of deer can be seen. The road east from Bridge of Balgie continues to the interesting old town of Aberfeldy, passing over a five-arched bridge built by General Wade in 1733. Close by is the Birks of Aberfeldy nature trail that follows the wild ravine of the Falls of Moness.

*Walkers enjoy the scenery
around Loch Katrine and
Ben Venue*

*View towards Tyndrum and
surrounding mountains*

Loch Lomond from Inversnaid, on the north-east shore

*Crieff, one of the gateways
to the Highlands, bedecked
in autumn colours*

*The beautiful Falls of
Dochart at Killin*

*Callander, with the River
Teith in the foreground and
Ben Ledi beyond*

*General Wade's bridge over
the River Tay at Aberfeldy*

Argyll and the Isles

Argyll, in Strathclyde, is the most southerly part of the Highlands, with perhaps some of the finest scenery to be found anywhere in Scotland; it is not only the islands that make it such an exciting place to visit, but the very nature of its unspoilt terrain.

Coming from Crianlarich on the A82 from Glasgow, the road bears left at the busy junction of Tyndrum to join the A85 for Oban, while the A82 continues on through Glencoe to Fort William. The A85 passes through Glen Lochy on the way to the village of Dalmally, which is near Kilchurn Castle, a stronghold of the Campbells. (Incidentally, the West Highland Railway line also follows this scenic route to Oban.) Kilchurn Castle lies in a commanding position on a small peninsula at the head of Loch Awe. Originally the castle consisted only of a tower or keep, built in the fifteenth century by Sir Colin Campbell of Glen Orchy. In 1693 it was enlarged into a castle with a surrounding wall by the 1st Earl of Breadalbane, whose wife was a Campbell; their initials are carved on the lintel over the entrance to the castle. During the Jacobite Rebellion of 1745, the castle was garrisoned by Hanoverian troops.

Near this imposing castle ruin is the Cruachan Dam Visitors' Centre, which offers a fascinating experience. A viewing gallery inside the mountain allows visitors to see the turbine hall in which electricity is generated from water fed 1,195 ft (364.5 m) down from the upper reservoir. There is a delightful picnic area next to Loch Awe, and across the road are the lovely Falls of Cruachan.

At Lochawe village, by the pier, cruises are available in the summer season on the *Lady Rowena*, around the many islands of Loch Awe. The road continues through the Pass of Brander, where the mighty twin-peaked Ben Cruachan, with its majestic presence and height of over 3,700 ft (1,127 m) overshadows the whole area.

Beyond the pass is the remote sea loch, Loch Etive. From here the only way to reach the head of the loch is by steamer: pleasure boats run during the summer, and details are available from Oban tourist office. At one time the steamer was the only means for transporting coal and other commodities to the crofters, who gathered at the pier at the head of the loch from remote outlying crofts.

From the pier a byroad runs through Glen Etive, winding and twisting along a mountainous route until it meets the main road through Glen Coe. The remote Glen Etive is home of the golden eagle, a majestic bird with a 6½-8 ft (1.9-2.4 m) wing span, which soars above the mountains, sometimes diving at incredible speed to catch its prey, at other times circling the sky effortlessly. Deer roam this wild country too, keeping their young out of sight, high up in the sheltered parts of the mountains, until they are able to fend for themselves.

Before reaching the busy town of Oban, take the Fort William road over the Connel Bridge, where there is spectacular scenery. About 10 miles (16 km) further on, by the shore of the sea loch, Loch Creran, is the Sea Life Centre, which is ideal for families. The centre provides an interesting experience with its displays of rare sea fish, and its seals, which can be seen at feeding time.

Kilchurn Castle, at the head of Loch Awe

The principal town of Oban is the connecting link for ferry services to the islands. Mull is the largest island and has a frequent ferry service, especially in the summer months; it is a direct link to the remote and lovely Isle of Iona, where St Columba established Christianity in the sixth century. Close to Iona on the Isle of Staffa is Fingal's Cave, which is 230 feet (69 m) deep and 60 feet (18 m) high. The cave was immortalised by Mendelssohn in his inspiring *Hebrides* overture, but the whole island is quite spectacular, with its huge basalt columns rising out of the turbulent sea. Two excellent boats run from Iona to Staffa throughout the summer months, and it is possible to land on the island when the weather is fine.

Another ferry service from Mull at Fishnish crosses the Sound of Mull to Lochaline, on the south end of Morven. The route to Fort William from here passes through magnificent countryside. On the coastal road, at Corran, there is a ferry service across Loch Linnhe to Onich, where the A82 leads to Fort William in one direction and to Glencoe via the Ballachulish Bridge in the other.

To discover Argyll by another route, take the ferry steamer from Gourock, some 20 miles (32 km) west of Glasgow, to Dunoon, or better still if time allows, catch the ferry from Ardrossan in Ayrshire and sail up the beautiful waters of the Clyde, landing at Rothesay on the Isle of Bute. At the northern end of the island a small ferry crosses the Kyles of Bute to the mainland; the route to Dunoon from here is incomparable for the grandeur of its scenery.

From Lochranza on the Isle of Arran there is a ferry service in the summer months to Claonaig on the Kintyre Peninsula - yet another way to enter Argyll. Running south from Claonaig is a magical road along the coast to Campbeltown; however, for ferries to the Isles of Islay and Jura it is necessary to go to West Loch Tarbert or Tarbert.

North of Tarbert the A83 passes Lochgilphead on the way to Inveraray, where there is much to see besides Inveraray Castle, the seat of the Duke of Argyll. A great attraction is the Jail, where there is a reconstruction of days gone by, when it was in very different use. The courtroom is just how it used to be, with life-like figures to represent the law. Beyond Inveraray a byroad through Hell's Glen leads to Lochgoilhead and the European Sheep and Wool Centre. Many breeds of sheep are shown in a demonstration that is quite unique.

At Oban, Caledonian MacBrayne's latest ferry, the *Lord of the Isles*, runs a service to the remoter Isles of Col and Tiree, and the Western Isles.

Inside Scottish Power's Cruachan Power Station

The busy port of Oban, a major ferry terminus

Attractive colour-washed buildings line the waterfront at Tobermory, the 'capital' of Mull
Historic Iona Abbey

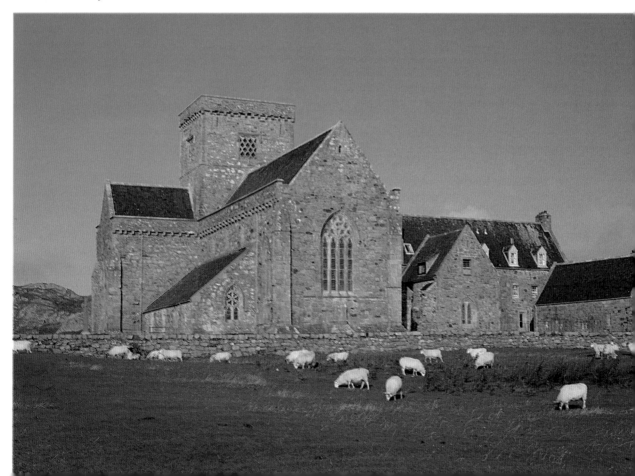

Fingal's Cave on the Isle of Staffa, inspiration for the composer Mendelssohn

Inveraray Castle, one of the principal attractions in the west of Scotland

Ferry entering Rothesay harbour, Isle of Bute

Rural landscape near Brodick, Arran

Glen Coe and Fort William

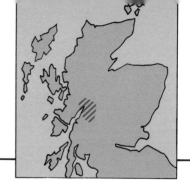

Glen Coe in Argyll is surrounded by formidable mountain ranges and vast stretches of bleak moorland. The Buachaille Etive mountain guards the entrance to the glen; the name means 'the Great Shepherd of Etive'. The superb ski slopes at the White Corries, close to King's House Hotel, have recently been extended and improved. A bigger chair-lift has been installed, and the facilities have been improved for greater enjoyment in both winter and summer.

In this beautiful area mountain peaks tower above the road in awesome grandeur. The Three Sisters of Glencoe are sometimes hidden by mist, but on a clear day they are most distinctive, as is the ridge of Aonach Eagach, close to the National Trust for Scotland's centre. The Trust cares for more than 14,000 acres (5,660 ha) of Glen Coe, and the centre is an excellent place to obtain information on the glen and its history. There is also a ranger who organises walks up into the mountains which are a paradise for climbers. The mountains in Glen Coe can be extremely dangerous and must be respected; the weather can change so rapidly that it is easy to get lost – many accidents happen every year. Near the centre is a Forestry Commission camp site, and there are several other camp sites in the glen.

Glen Coe continues to Loch Leven, which is surrounded by mountains. Glencoe village has not changed much over the years, but Ballachulish Bridge is comparatively new. Before it was built there was a ferry service operating across Loch Leven to nearby Fort William, otherwise it was necessary to go via Kinlochleven at the head of the loch, incidentally a delightful detour.

The present town of Fort William developed largely after the coming of the railway in the nineteenth century – the original government fortress of 1655, rebuilt by General Wade in 1724, was demolished in 1864 to make way for the station. A special steam train runs to Fort William by the West Highland Line's scenic route which ends at Mallaig, with ferry connections to the Isle of Skye. Just outside Fort William on the way to Spean Bridge and the Great Glen is a narrow, winding byroad leading to the foot of Ben Nevis through the superb scenery of Glen Nevis. A footpath continues through to Rannoch Moor. There are several camp sites in the glen for the many visitors who come to enjoy this beautiful mountainous area.

Four miles north of Fort William on the Spean Bridge road is Nevis Range, situated on the 4,006 ft (1,221 m) Aonach Mór mountain beside Ben Nevis, with the only Alpine gondola system in Britain. It is open all year except November, and provides an up-to-date ski area with seven ski lifts and the longest ski-run in Scotland (over 1.2 miles/2 km). Additional attractions in this mountain area are ranger-guided climbs and waymarked paths to enable nature lovers to get a closer glimpse of the wildlife, wild flowers, corries and forests of the mountains, the highest in Britain. 'No-go' areas are clearly marked to help protect the environment.

On the A830 'Road to the Isles' at Corpach is the Treasures of the Earth centre, where Europe's finest gemstone and crystal collection is displayed in a stunning simulation of cave, cavern and mining scenes. Priceless gemstones and beautiful crystals are set against a scenic backdrop of ancient forests and tumbling waterfalls.

At Lochy Bridge on the outskirts of Fort William is the Ben Nevis Distillery, where 'The Legend of the Dew of Ben Nevis' may be discovered at the visitors' centre. In 1825 'Long John' MacDonald opened the distillery in the shadow of Ben Nevis, where the source of the waters is so pure and rare that the quality is unsurpassable, hence the whisky's branded name, 'The Legend of the Dew of Ben Nevis'. Incidentally, the Gaelic name for whisky is *Uisge Beatha*, meaning 'the water of life'.

Walkers explore the haunting mountain scenery of Glen Coe

Buachaille Etive Mór at the entrance of Glen Etive

Morning mist encircles the Three Sisters of Glencoe

Loch Leven at Ballachulish

*A West Highland Line steam
train near Glenfinnan Viaduct*

*The Water of Nevis flowing
through scenic Glen Nevis*

Restaurant and gondola top station, Nevis Range, near Fort William

For its unique display of gemstones and crystals, the Treasures of the Earth centre at Corpach has won the Scottish Tourist Board's 'Thistle' award for tourism

Ben Nevis Distillery, Lochy Bridge

Glen Shiel and the 'Road to the Isles'

The A87 road through Glen Shiel to Kyle of Lochalsh is one of the two 'Roads to the Isles' to Skye and the Western Isles (the other is the winding A830 to Mallaig from Fort William). Glen Shiel in Ross-shire is a wildly picturesque glen, dominated by the mountains of the Five Sisters of Kintail and the Saddle. Its beauty is enhanced by the lochs that receive the water cascading down the mountain gullies. There are two main lochs in the glen lying close to the road, Loch Cluanie at the start of the glen, and the sea loch, Loch Duich, at the end, which converges with Loch Long and Loch Alsh, also sea lochs.

Near Loch Cluanie, which has a viewpoint on its dam, is an old coaching inn in a superb position for travellers and climbers. Cluanie Inn is within easy-commuting distance of Inverness, Fort William, Fort Augustus and Drumnadrochit; not far to the west is Kyle of Lochalsh, where frequent ferries run to the Isle of Skye. Herds of red deer roam the hills near the inn, and at dusk they come down to feed in the glen, drinking from the mountain streams. Because their colouring blends so well with the surroundings, the deer are more easily seen when they move. The rutting season is in October, and to be fortunate enough to hear their eerie bellowing cries ringing through the mountains, as the stags fight for the supremacy of the herd, is a great thrill and something that will remain locked in the memory forever.

The most photographed castle in Scotland must be Eilean Donan Castle at Dornie. This was once a fort, replaced in the thirteenth century by a castle with a great encircling wall. In the fourteenth century it fell into the hands of the Earl of Moray, who was a cruel, heartless landlord. A grisly incident is recorded which demonstrates his barbarism. To teach the local inhabitants a lesson, and to show them who was master, he had fifty of them slaughtered and hung their heads, which slowly decayed, on the castle wall for all to see. Now the famous castle is the stronghold of the Clan MacRae, and houses the Clan MacRae war memorial.

The castle lies at the mouth of Loch Duich, overlooked by Beinn a' Chùirn and the distant mountains of Glen Shiel. It is approached by a causeway, and over the entrance doorway, carved in the stonework, is a Gaelic inscription which translates as: 'While there's a MacRae within there will never be a Fraser without'. In 1719 the castle was largely destroyed; restoration work began in 1912 and was completed in 1932. The castle became floodlit in 1990, adding considerably to its romantic appeal. On a clear day it is a truly magnificent sight to see it reflected in Loch Duich, especially if there is a white mist kissing the mountain tops, when it looks just like a fairy castle.

Plockton, a favourite mecca for yachtsmen, is in the care of the National Trust for Scotland and lies further west in a very sheltered bay by the sea loch, Loch Carron. All along the narrow coastal road the scenery is superb.

Glenelg is south-west of Kyle of Lochalsh, on the Sound of Sleat. In the summer season a small ferry to the Isle of Skye operates from this delightful village, tucked away in a remote corner of the Highlands. From the Sound of Sleat two sea lochs, Loch Hourn and Loch Nevis, enter the mainland, penetrating some beautiful, isolated country which is ideal for walkers. The two lochs offer quite an adventure for yachtsmen to explore in the summer. At the head of Loch Hourn is a byroad to Glen Garry that meets the main road from Inverness to Fort William. Loch Nevis, however, Europe's deepest sea loch, is more remote, although it can be reached by a passenger ferry service from Glenelg to Mallaig. No roads cover this distance, but a byroad from Glenelg follows a scenic mountainous route to Shiel Bridge.

Glen Shiel and the Saddle

Bernera, near Glenelg, lies in a picturesque setting south-west of Kyle of Lochalsh

The wild beauty of Loch Cluanie

Ancient Eilean Donan Castle, near Dornie,
is linked to the shore by a causeway

Loch Duich, overlooked by the magnificent
snow-capped Five Sisters of Kintail

The sheltered harbour at Plockton

Beautiful coastal scenery surrounds the sea loch, Loch Carron

Tranquil Loch Hourn – an adventure for yachtsmen in summer

The South-west Highlands

The south-west Highlands lie roughly within the Loch Alsh and Wester Ross regions, an area of great solitude and isolation, with mysterious mountain ranges, wide open glens and beautiful lochs. At the head of Loch Long is the path for the Falls of Glomach. The walk is 7 miles (11 km) long and very arduous; it is unwise to attempt it alone. But the rewards are great if conditions are safe, and you are adventurous enough to accept the challenge of getting there! Allow at least eight hours to get there and back. The falls are perhaps the most spectacular in Britain, and though not the highest, have the biggest single drop of 370 feet (111 m). If the wind is right you can hear the roar of the waterfall long before you reach it. A less arduous 5-mile (8 km) walk leads from Dorusduain car park, close to the National Trust for Scotland's adventure school at Morvich, and takes five hours in total.

At Torridon the Trust operates an audio-visual and photographic display of wildlife, and a ranger organises guided walks. The Trust cares for 16,000 acres (6,500 ha) in an estate that has some of the finest scenery in the Highlands. One of the most awe-inspiring walks is the Torridon Walk, from Achnashellach railway station to Torridon: the trail follows rivers and lochs, and runs between two great mountains, Beinn Liath Mhór and Maol Chean-dearg, both over 3,000 feet (900 m) high. Also in the Trust's care are the beautiful Balgy Falls at the end of Loch Damh, near the sea loch of Upper Loch Torridon. Loch Damh is an isolated inland loch of considerable length, overlooked by Ben Shieldaig on one side and Beinn Damh on the other.

The Trust cares for a bird sanctuary at Loch Shieldaig, and there is a deer nature reserve at Loch Carron and another near Glen Shieldaig. However, the largest reserve is the Beinn Eighe National Nature Reserve by Kinlochewe, where red deer, golden eagles, pine martens and wild cats can be seen. This was the first national nature reserve to be set up in Great Britain.

In this part of the south-west Highlands there is one route that will particularly appeal to the adventurous. It runs off the A896 near Kishorn, through the Pass of the Cattle (Bealch nam Bo) on a narrow mountainous road of steep hairpin bends and sudden dips with 1-in-4 gradients, until it descends from 2,054 feet (616 m) to level out, and suddenly Applecross appears in all its isolated glory of sandy beaches and quiet solitude.

The narrow coastal road north of Applecross twists, dips and climbs relentlessly along a memorable route to Shieldaig, a village tucked under the mountains on the shores of Loch Shieldaig. The atmosphere of quiet relaxation to be found here is perfect for unwinding from the cares of the world.

The spectacular Falls of Glomach, at the head of Loch Long

The crystal blue waters of Loch Torridon

Loch Shieldaig, framed by picturesque woodland

The snowy peaks of Beinn Eighe

Applecross was once known as the most inaccessible place on the Scottish mainland

The Hebridean Isles: Skye & the Western Isles

The Isle of Skye, in the Inner Hebrides, is very much part of the Scottish Highlands. The 'Misty Isle' of mysterious mountains and long, fertile peninsulas has a way of life that is foreign to city-dwellers and commercial entrepreneurs. Crofting is still very much in operation, and the fishing industry is also important. It is true that many islanders depend on the tourist trade and have adapted to it well, but there are no signs that the island has been spoilt by it. The islanders are very proud of their heritage.

The main mountain range is the Cuillin Hills, or Black Cuillins, and climbers come from around the world to pit their strength against these gigantic peaks. This mountain range lies in the south-west of the island, yet its towering strength dominates the surrounding area. Excellent views can be seen from Elgol and Sligachan Bridge. The mist-shrouded peaks of the Red Cuillins, which are composed of pink granite, overlook the road to Portree from Kyleakin.

Skye's Heritage Centre, situated in the fresh air and beauty of Portree Forest, combines an imaginative exhibition of the history, culture and landscape of the island with a restaurant and a shop selling books and local crafts and music.

The A855 road from Portree offers a good view of the Storr, a dramatic 10 mile-long (16 km) mountain range, with rocks of unusual shapes; one is called the Old Man of Storr. There are also two waterfalls, the Lealt Falls and Gorge and the Kilt Rock Falls. The latter is a spectacular sight – Loch Mealt is the source of a river that flows under a bridge and then cascades down over a steep and dangerous cliff called Kilt Rock, a 170ft (51m) drop to the sea below.

Close to Staffin is the Quiraing, which is in golden eagle country. Weathering of the ancient landscape here has created a curious façade of rock pinnacles, grass-topped 'tables' and screes. The road to Uig from Staffin is very twisty with a particularly steep hairpin bend.

Near Kilmuir is a memorial cross to Flora MacDonald, the Jacobite heroine who saved Bonnie Prince Charles by disguising him as a woman and bringing him over to Skye from the Western Isles. Also located here is the Skye Museum of Island Life, where there are several beautifully restored thatched croft houses depicting life as it was long ago.

To reach Uig, further along the coast road, from Kilmuir it is necessary to negotiate a series of steep hairpin bends, but the views at the top are superb. It is at Uig that Caledonian MacBrayne's ferry service operates for the Western Isles.

The A856 road south from Uig meets up with the A850 Dunvegan road, which winds along the coast for part of the way. Dunvegan Castle is the home of the MacLeods of MacLeod, and is an ancient, interesting castle. The sea loch, Loch Dunvegan, is a favourite haunt for grey seals, which

sometimes call to each other across the water, an unforgettable sound. The road south from Dunvegan eventually joins the Kyleakin road at Sligachan Bridge, where the mysterious Cuillin Hills may once again be glimpsed. Beyond the bridge, tucked away off the road at Luib, is another croft museum.

Following the Kyleakin road there is an interesting study centre for geologists at Broadford, where the road leads off to Elgol on the A881. Near Armadale is the Clan Donald Centre, a converted castle which houses a Museum of the Isles, audio-visual display and craft shop. In the spring the wooded wild gardens are covered in primroses and bluebells, a mantle of green falling over them from the trees above.

During the summer months the Armadale ferry runs from the Sleat Peninsula to Mallaig, a busy fishing harbour and tourist attraction on the mainland. Passengers alighting from the ferry are able to catch a connecting train to Fort William; this journey attracts many people because of the magnificent scenery and the special steam-haul train. By car the road passes mountains and lochs before reaching Glenfinnan, where there is a monument to Bonnie Prince Charles, in the care of the National Trust for Scotland.

The Western Isles, in the Outer Hebrides, have a beauty all of their own. Judging by the prehistoric monuments that can be found all over the islands, they have been inhabited for possibly 10,000 years.

Their beauty lies in their remoteness, which has prevented the modern rush of city life touching them, and hence it is a wonderful place to spend a holiday. The pace of life is much slower, ideal for unwinding and forgetting daily cares.

Golden sands with deep turquoise-blue waters adorn the coastlines. Nature reserves and bird sanctuaries provide an ideal setting for bird-watching, and the many wild flowers are a joy to behold. Wildlife abounds: hidden in their natural habitats, deer and seals can best be discovered on long walks or when exploring the beaches. There are so many beautiful islands – all different, and many off the beaten track – that the visitor will want to return again and again.

The principle islands are Barra and Vatersay, joined recently by a causeway; South Uist, Benbecula and North Uist, joined by two main causeways; and Harris and Lewis, joined by a main road from South Rodel, in the south of Harris, to the Butt of Lewis. Lewis is by far the largest island, where the famous prehistoric Callanish Stones can be found. These stones date back to 2,000 BC.

The major link to the mainland is by Caledonian MacBrayne's steamer ferry service, although there is a good airport at Benbecula. During the summer season Caledonian MacBrayne operates a 'Hopscotch' ticket which enables the visitor to make a round trip of the main islands. There are several places to start the journey and various routes to choose, but whichever way the experience will be unforgettable.

Fishing and crofting remain important to the islanders, whose native tongue is Gaelic, and weaving is still a cottage industry. Many smaller ferry boats, both for cars and for foot passengers, provide a necessary service for the other islands and allow visitors access to areas that would otherwise be denied them.

The weather is variable, but sometimes in May the sun can make the sand almost too hot to walk on, and often when conditions on the mainland are poor, these remote islands are bathed in sunshine for days on end. There are plenty of places to stay, with many good hotels and caravan sites.

The only large town in the Western Isles is Stornoway, on Lewis, which lies off Broad Bay. A beautiful river walk runs from Stornoway Castle, which dominates the town, to Gallows Hill, so-called because criminals used to be hanged there.

The ferry steamer leaves Stornoway for Ullapool on the mainland – its arrival and departure create quite a commotion, reminding the visitor that the islanders do indeed have a different way of life.

Cottages at Digg, on the Trotternish Peninsula, north-east Skye

A dramatic silhouette of the Cuillins. Inset: *The Skye Heritage Centre in beautiful Portree Forest*

Dunvegan Castle, seat of the Clan MacLeod and worldwide centre of reunion for members of the clan

A steep hairpin bend at the Quiraing, in golden eagle country

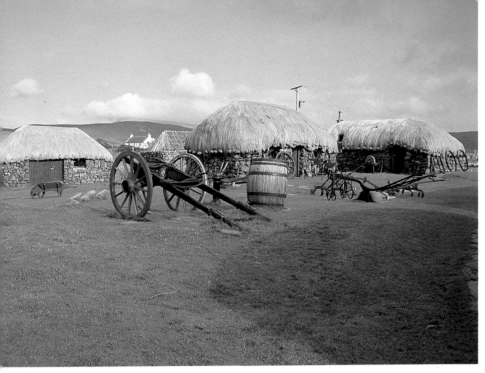

Among the exhibits at the Skye Museum of Island Life at Kilmuir are early domestic appliances and farming implements

Uig Bay - a ferry service operates from here to the Western Isles in the Outer Hebrides

*Pink tufts of the wild flower Thrift (*Armeria maritima*) may be seen among the coastal rocks of the Western Isles*

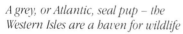

The white sandy bay at Seilebost, South Harris

A grey, or Atlantic, seal pup – the Western Isles are a haven for wildlife

Red deer stags battle for supremacy during the rutting season in October

The Western Highlands

The rugged coastline, massive mountain ranges, deep sea lochs and numerous small islands of the western Highlands, which lie within the Wester Ross and Sutherland regions, offer breathtaking views. Although the area receives more rain than the east coast it is nonetheless warmer by comparison.

From Gairloch to Ullapool the coastal route is wonderful, with impressive mountain ranges and wide open sea lochs. There are long stretches of sandy beaches and hidden bays that attract many campers in the summer months.

Inverewe Gardens, in the sheltered bay of Loch Ewe near Poolewe, are in fact quite sub-tropical. The gardens are in the care of the National Trust for Scotland and are an unexpected paradise in the midst of wilderness. In 1862 Osgood Mackenzie, with great vision and planning, proved that a sub-tropical garden could be grown out of red sandstone with a soil of acid peat, once it was enriched by blue clay from the shore and other soils; after the peat was well drained the miracle began to take shape. There are over 2,000 acres at Inverewe, where trees, shrubs and flowers from all over the world flourish in abundance. It took Osgood Mackenzie sixty years to finish this incredible feat, which the Trust so lovingly cares for now. He could not have envisaged the hundreds of thousands of people that come from all over the world to visit this amazing garden, many of whom return year after year.

Ullapool receives numerous foreign visitors from the ships and yachts that shelter in its harbour. Caledonian MacBrayne's ferry service goes to Stornoway from here, and a 'Hopscotch' ticket will take you down to Oban via the Western Isles.

A challenging, twisty road near Ullapool, close to the Inverpolly National Nature Reserve, climbs to Inverkirkaig (where there is an amazing bookshop full of surprises). Great care is required on this coastal byroad, which has fantastic scenery but is narrow and single-track. At Lochinver the main A837 road runs through the mountains, but the coastal road continues to Kylesku Bridge. Close to the bridge lies the highest waterfall in Britain, the Eas-Coul-Aulin waterfall, with a drop of 658 feet (197 m), three times higher than Niagara Falls.

A remote grandeur rests on this land, which is quite unlike anywhere else in the Scottish Highlands; the terrain is wilder and bleaker, but it is in this very remoteness and wild, undisturbed beauty that its great strength lies.

Loch Broom from Ardcharnich

The sheltered, sandy bay at Gairloch

Plants from all over the world flourish in the warm Gulf Stream climate at Inverewe Gardens

Isolated Sandwood Bay, north of Kinlochbervie, is famed for its unspoilt scenery

A rainbow arcs over fishing boats in the busy port and holiday resort of Ullapool

The spectacular Eas-Coul-Aulin waterfall, near Kylesku

Inverness and around the A9

Inverness is the capital of the Scottish Highlands, lying at the mouth of the River Ness on the Moray Firth coast. Inverness Castle was built around 1840 as a sheriff court and jail; it stands high over the River Ness, and a small centre in the castle is open to the public.

Inverness is in a central position for exploring the Highlands; Ullapool, for example, on the west coast, is only 55 miles (88 km) away. In recent years much has been accomplished to improve road communications. Kessock Bridge opened in 1982 to replace the small ferry service that operated across the Beauly Firth to the Black Isle. The Cromarty Bridge was opened in 1979, crossing the Cromarty Firth from the Black Isle, and the new Dornoch Bridge over the Dornoch Firth completes the improvements, giving Inverness a direct route to Wick and Thurso. Inverness Airport runs services to Aberdeen, the Western Isles, Orkney and Shetland, commuting with Edinburgh, Glasgow and London.

The greatest attraction close to Inverness is Loch Ness, and a road goes all the way round the loch. A good place to start is on the less frequented side, at Dores, passing the beautiful falls at Foyers to the south. At Fort Augustus the road meets up with the main A82 Inverness to Fort William road. The Benedictine Abbey at Fort Augustus was built in 1876 on the site of the fort which General Wade constructed in the eighteenth century as an army communications point for Fort William and Fort George. The fort was pulled down to receive the abbey. Visitors are welcome in the extensive grounds. On the way back to Inverness from Fort Augustus the road passes Urquhart Castle and Drumnadrochit, where there is the official Loch Ness Monster Exhibition. There have been many sightings of the Loch Ness Monster near Urquhart Castle.

A few miles south-east of Inverness is the Culloden battlefield, cared for by the National Trust for Scotland, where there is an audio-visual centre. Close by is Cawdor Castle, the seat of the Campbells of Cawdor, which is open to the public. On the Moray coast is the magnificent Fort George, and there are many good golf-courses and sandy beaches near Nairn.

Be sure to visit the Cromarty Court House visitors' centre on the Black Isle, just north of Inverness. The building dates from 1773, and on show are animated figures, the first of their kind in Scotland. There is also a taped 'tour' of Cromarty, where the famous geologist Hugh Miller was born. To venture further north, follow the coast road to Dunrobin Castle at Golspie. The castle is the historic seat of the earls and dukes of Sutherland. The massive inner keep was built in 1275, and the main structure a century later. Over the years many further structural changes have been made, but it has always remained a Sutherland possession. At Helmsdale there is an interesting museum called 'Timespan', depicting the Clearances and early Highland life. The A9 continues along the rocky coastline to Dunbeath, which has a remarkable heritage centre, well worth visiting. Beyond is the lively town of Wick, and then John o' Groats, famous for its coupling with Land's End in England, and where the 'Last House in Scotland' has a fine museum. Close by is Gills, where there is a new ferry terminal for Orkney. The Queen Mother's Castle of Mey is between John o' Groats and Thurso, near Dunnet Head, the most northerly point in the British Isles.

The extensive coastline runs across the northern Highlands from John o' Groats to Durness and is full of beautiful sandy bays and high, rocky cliffs. Although the Sutherland coast is a very isolated area there are three good roads running inland: from Bettyhill, above a vast sandy bay; from Tongue, lying above the causeway that crosses the Kyles of Tongue; and from Durness near the Smoo Caves and several golden bays. The three roads converge at Lairg by Loch Shin, close to the remarkable Falls of Shin. The road from Lairg passes over Bonar Bridge to Alness, not far from Inverness.

South of Inverness there are numerous places to visit, clearly signposted off the A9. For example, the Landmark Centre at Carrbridge, with its many interesting nature trails; Kincraig Wildlife Park, which is associated with the Edinburgh Zoo; the Aviemore Centre, a massive complex of entertainment and sporting activities; and the Strathspey Railway, which operates an exciting steam train journey between Boat of Garten and Aviemore. Further south is Blair Castle, home of the Duke of Atholl, set within fine parklands, where there is a campsite. Killiecrankie is where the Jacobites fought and won a battle in 1689; one soldier escaped by leaping across the gorge. The River Garry gushes through the wooded ravine, and waymarked walks lead down the deep gorge – the whole area is under the care of the National Trust for Scotland.

Not far from here is the delightful town of Pitlochry, an ideal place to stay as it is in a central position for visiting the many places of interest in the area, such as the Pitlochry Dam Visitors' Centre with its fish-ladder, which was created when the River Tummel was dammed by a hydroelectric scheme in the 1950s. Behind a glass panel is a viewing-chamber constructed underwater, which allows visitors to see salmon negotiating the specially constructed ladder, which passes under the dam. The salmon then make their way to the man-made Loch Faskally and on towards their spawning-grounds. An audio-visual programme gives a detailed guide to this interesting complex.

Just outside Pitlochry, where the Pitlochry Festival Theatre operates a full programme with a Highland night every Monday, there are two Scotch whisky distilleries. Edradour Distillery, which claims to be the smallest distillery in Scotland, was established in 1825 and lies in an attractive situation east of the town. The Blair Athol Distillery is part of United Distillers, which operates a large number of distilleries throughout the Highlands, with many visitors' centres.

From Pitlochry it is easy to commute to the nearby Forestry Commission Centre at the Queen's View, so-called because Queen Victoria was entranced with the panoramic view over Loch Tummel to Schiehallion, and beyond to far-off Glen Coe. The Hermitage at Dunkeld lies south of Pitlochry, off the A9, amidst the waterfalls and rapids of the River Braan, a splendid walking area.

Many rural towns lie around and about Pitlochry, for example, Blairgowrie, Aberfeldy, Kirkmichael, Dunkeld and the conservation village of Moulin, where a church has stood for more than 1,400 years. The historic city of Perth, with its many attractions, is less than 30 miles (48 km) off the A9 to the south.

The Scottish Highlands are one of the last remaining wildernesses in Europe, where nature is still more in control than man. If all goes well, this will always be so.

Inverness Castle dominates the mouth of the River Ness

Fort Augustus, a former Hanoverian outpost against insurgent Jacobite Highlanders

The Loch Ness Monster Exhibition Centre, Drumnadrochit

Culloden Moor, where Bonnie Prince Charles' Jacobite army was defeated by the Duke of Cumberland in 1746

Wick was once an important herring fishing and curing centre. The name comes from the Norse word vik *meaning 'bay'*

Sandy bays backed by rich pastures near Durness, on the northern Highland coast

The scenic Falls of Shin, near Lairg, a pretty resort on Loch Shin

The Scottish baronial-style elegance of Blair Castle, Blair Atholl

Further information

Various conservation societies have been formed to protect and preserve Scotland's heritage. The largest is the National Trust for Scotland, which since 1931 has pledged its commitment to maintain and protect the nation's architectural, scenic and historic treasures in its care, and to encourage public enjoyment of them. The Trust, an independent charity, depends for its support on donations and subscriptions from members. It now cares for over a hundred properties and 100,000 acres (40,000 ha) of countryside. It is also associated with Scotland's Garden Scheme and ranger/naturalist service.

The Forestry Commission is a government body responsible for seeing that large areas of Scotland, especially the Highlands, are forested for present and future generations. The Commission provides many recreational facilities, including waymarked forest walks, nature trails, picnic sites, camp sites and visitors' centres, including the Queen Elizabeth Forest Park and an audio-visual centre at the Queen's View, near Pitlochry.

The imposing ruins of Urquhart Castle, overlooking Loch Ness

Sunset from Fort George

Historic Scotland cares for 330 sites of ancient monuments and buildings throughout Scotland. In the Scottish Highlands there is the Dallas Dhu distillery, south of Forres, a completely preserved 'time capsule' of the distiller's craft. Not far from here is Fort George, which was built as a fortress following the battle of Culloden. It is one of the outstanding artillery fortifications in Europe and still an active army barracks, covering 42 acres (17 ha) and enclosed by 1 mile (1.6 km) of ramparts. Urquhart Castle, on a rocky promontory in Loch Ness, near Drumnadrochit, is one of the largest castles in the Highlands. Thirteenth-century Kildrummy Castle, near Alford, on the Castle Trail, is known as the 'Queen of Highland Castles'.

On behalf of the Scottish people, Parliament has charged Scottish Natural Heritage with the duty of protecting and enhancing Scotland's natural heritage – the wildlife, habitats and landscapes which have evolved in Scotland through the long partnership between people and nature. Scottish Natural Heritage's aim is to enable people to enjoy the natural heritage, understand it and use it wisely 'in a manner which is sustainable'. The organisation's founding legislation, the Natural Heritage (Scotland) Act 1991, enshrines the word 'sustainable' for the first time in UK legislation.

The historic Pass of Killiecrankie, site of the amazing Soldier's Leap

Observation chambers at Pitlochry Dam allow visitors to watch the passage of salmon up-river to their spawning grounds

Named after Queen Victoria, the Queen's View over Loch Tummel is one of the grandest glen views in Scotland